THE Nonreligious BEST QUOTES EVER

a portable collection of uplifting and humorous nonreligious quotes

Christine Pierce and Kevin Reedy

Now What PRESS, LLC
Lake Oswego, Oregon

Copyright © 2008 by Christine Pierce and Kevin Reedy

All rights reserved. All quotations remain the intellectual property of their respective originators. We do not assert any claim of copyright for individual quotations. No part of this book may be reproduced, stored in a retrieval system or transmitted in any form or by any means without the prior written permission of the publisher; exceptions are made for brief excerpts used in published reviews.

Published by

Now What PRESS, LLC
333 S. State Street, Suite #172
Lake Oswego, OR 97034
http://NowWhatPress.com

ISBN: 978-0-9663742-3-0
LCCN: 2008905342

Printed in the United States of America.

Disclaimer: To the best of our knowledge, all quotations included here fall under the fair use or public domain guidelines of copyright law in the United States. If you believe that any quotation violates a copyright you hold or represent, we will remove it from any future editions upon notification pending good-faith resolution of any dispute.

We strive for accuracy but cannot be held liable or responsible for any errors in quotations or incorrect attributions. By quoting authors we do not in any way mean to imply their endorsement or approval of our book or its contents.

If you discover an error, please let us know by visiting our website at www.nowwhatpress.com.

CONTENTS

Anxiety and Stress 1
Beauty... 7
Courage.................................. 13
Death 19
Enthusiasm 27
Forgiveness 35
Friendship 41
Happiness 47
Honor..................................... 55
Hope 61
Humor 67
Kindness 77
Love 85
Meaning and Purpose 91
Nature 99
Parenting 107
Peace 113
Perseverance 117
Reason 127
Responsibility 135
Simplicity............................. 143
Tolerance 149

INTRODUCTION

Everyone enjoys a good quote. Well-turned phrases can make us pause to reflect or inspire us to action. A book of quotes is a great way to find the right sentiment for the right time.

Surprisingly, few (if any) inspirational quote books have been compiled without any religious references. Until now. *The Best Nonreligious Quotes Ever* provides encouraging, thoughtful, and often humorous quotations of a nonreligious nature.

This innovative book features quotations from a wide selection of people, both famous and not-so-famous. These quotes can be used for personal inspiration, or readily sprinkled into speeches, toasts and conversations.

We hope these quotations will be a source of pleasure and encouragement. We also know there are more great nonreligious quotes out there. We welcome your input. If you'd like to share your favorite quotes with us, or see our growing collection, please visit our website, www.nonreligiousquotes.com.

ANXIETY AND STRESS

A crust eaten in peace is better than a banquet partaken in anxiety.

AESOP

Much of the stress that people feel doesn't come from having too much to do. It comes from not finishing what they've started.

DAVID ALLEN

If you worried about falling off the bike, you'd never get on.

LANCE ARMSTRONG

THE BEST *Nonreligious* QUOTES EVER

Give a man a fish and he will eat for a day.
Teach him how to fish,
and he will sit in a boat and drink beer all day.

GEORGE CARLIN

We have a lot of anxieties, and one cancels out another very often.

WINSTON CHURCHILL

Do not anticipate trouble, or worry about what may never happen. Keep in the sunlight.

BENJAMIN FRANKLIN

A mistake in judgment isn't fatal,
but too much anxiety about judgment is.

PAULINE KAEL

Neither comprehension nor learning can take place in an atmosphere of anxiety.

ROSE KENNEDY

ANXIETY AND STRESS

I don't have big anxieties. I wish I did.
I'd be much more interesting.

ROY LICHTENSTEIN

The best thing one can do when it's raining
is to let it rain.

HENRY WADSWORTH LONGFELLOW

When all you own is a hammer,
every problem starts looking like a nail.

ABRAHAM MASLOW

Concentration is a fine antidote to anxiety.

JACK NICKLAUS

There is no such thing as pure pleasure;
some anxiety always goes with it.

OVID

THE BEST *Nonreligious* QUOTES EVER

Anxiety is a thin stream of fear trickling through the mind. If encouraged, it cuts a channel into which all other thoughts are drained.

ARTHUR SOMERS ROCHE

There are more things to alarm us than to harm us, and we suffer more often in apprehension than reality.

SENECA

There is nothing in the dark that isn't there when the lights are on.

ROD SERLING

The bow too tensely strung is easily broken.

PUBLIUS SYRUS

I've had thousands of problems in my life, most of which never actually happened.

MARK TWAIN

ANXIETY AND STRESS

The suspense is terrible, I hope it will last.

OSCAR WILDE

I try not to worry about the future —
so I take each day just one anxiety attack at a time.

TOM WILSON

Some people, no matter how old they get,
never lose their beauty — they merely move it
from their faces into their hearts.

MARTIN BUXBAUM

Beauty is unbearable, drives us to despair,
offering us for a minute the glimpse of an eternity
that we should like to stretch out over
the whole of time.

ALBERT CAMUS

Those who contemplate the beauty of the earth
find reserves of strength that will endure
as long as life lasts.

RACHEL CARSON

THE BEST *Nonreligious* QUOTES EVER

When you have only two pennies left in the world,
buy a loaf of bread with one,
and a lily with the other.

CHINESE PROVERB

Everything has its beauty, but not everyone sees it.

CONFUCIUS

Though we travel the world over to find
the beautiful, we must carry it with us
or we find it not.

RALPH WALDO EMERSON

As we grow old, the beauty steals inward.

RALPH WALDO EMERSON

When I am working on a problem I never
think about beauty. I only think about how to solve
the problem. But when I have finished,
if the solution is not beautiful,
I know it is wrong.

BUCKMINSTER FULLER

BEAUTY

If you can't make it good, at least make it look good.

BILL GATES

Time is a great healer, but a poor beautician.

LUCILLE S. HARPER

Beauty is no quality in things themselves:
it exists merely in the mind
which contemplates them.

DAVID HUME

Anyone who keeps the ability to see beauty
never grows old.

FRANZ KAFKA

A thing of beauty is a joy forever.

JOHN KEATS

The best and most beautiful things in the world
cannot be seen or even touched.
They must be felt with the heart.

HELEN KELLER

THE BEST *Nonreligious* QUOTES EVER

Beauty isn't worth thinking about;
what's important is your mind.
You don't want a fifty-dollar haircut
on a fifty-cent head.

GARRISON KEILLOR

I'm tired of all this nonsense about beauty
being only skin-deep. That's deep enough.
What do you want — an adorable pancreas?

JEAN KERR

That which is striking and beautiful is
not always good, but that which is good
is always beautiful.

NINON DE L'ENCLOS

Have nothing in your house
that you do not know to be useful,
or believe to be beautiful.

WILLIAM MORRIS

BEAUTY

Beauty is only skin deep,
but ugly goes clean to the bone.

DOROTHY PARKER

Remember that the most beautiful things
in the world are the most useless;
peacocks and lilies, for example.

JOHN RUSKIN

Taking joy in living is a woman's best cosmetic.

ROSALIND RUSSELL

A morning-glory at my window satisfies me
more than the metaphysics of books.

WALT WHITMAN

It's beauty that captures your attention;
personality which captures your heart.

AUTHOR UNKNOWN

THE BEST *Nonreligious* QUOTES EVER

I've never seen a smiling face
that was not beautiful.

AUTHOR UNKNOWN

Courage is simply the willingness
to be afraid and act anyway.

ROBERT ANTHONY

It is a wise man who knows where
courage ends and stupidity begins

JEROME CADY

Most of us have far more courage than
we ever dreamed we possessed.

DALE CARNEGIE

THE BEST *Nonreligious* QUOTES EVER

Life can be wonderful if you're not afraid of it.
All it takes is courage, imagination . . .
and a little dough.

CHARLIE CHAPLIN

When you see what is right,
have the courage to do it.

CHINESE PROVERB.

This is no time for ease and comfort.
It is the time to dare and endure.

WINSTON CHURCHILL

It takes courage to grow up and
become who you really are.

E. E. CUMMINGS

All our dreams can come true,
if we have the courage to pursue them.

WALT DISNEY

COURAGE

There is no victory at bargain basement prices.

DWIGHT D. EISENHOWER

A hero is no braver than an ordinary man,
but he is braver five minutes longer.

RALPH WALDO EMERSON

You don't develop courage by being happy in
your relationships everyday. You develop it
by surviving difficult times and
challenging adversity.

EPICURUS

Either life entails courage,
or it ceases to be life.

E.M. FORSTER

To me, there is no greater act of courage
than being the one who kisses first.

JANEANE GAROFALO

THE BEST *Nonreligious* QUOTES EVER

What would life be if we had no courage to attempt anything?

VINCENT VAN GOGH

Courage is very important. Like a muscle, it is strengthened by use.

RUTH GORDON

It is playing safe that we create a world of utmost insecurity.

DAG HAMMARSKJOLD

Courage is grace under pressure.

ERNEST HEMINGWAY

The greatest test of courage on earth is to bear defeat without losing heart.

ROBERT G. INGERSOLL

One man with courage makes a majority.

ANDREW JACKSON

COURAGE

Life is either a daring adventure or nothing.
HELEN KELLER

It is from numberless diverse acts of courage and belief that human history is shaped.
ROBERT F. KENNEDY

To face despair and not give in to it, that's courage.
TED KOPPEL

The only courage that matters is the kind that gets you from one moment to the next.
MIGNON MCLAUGHLIN

Life shrinks or expands in proportion to one's courage.
ANAIS NIN

To fear to face an issue is to believe the worst is true.
AYN RAND

THE BEST *Nonreligious* QUOTES EVER

Life is not meant to be easy, my child;
but take courage: it can be delightful.

GEORGE BERNARD SHAW

Courage is not the towering oak
that sees storms come and go;
it is the fragile blossom that opens in the snow.

ALICE MACKENZIE SWAIM

Courage is resistance to fear, mastery of fear —
not absence of fear.

MARK TWAIN

Courage is being scared to death —
but saddling up anyway.

JOHN WAYNE

Courage is the art of being the only one who knows
you're scared to death.

HAROLD WILSON

It's not that I'm afraid to die.
I just don't want to be there when it happens.

WOODY ALLEN

Life is pleasant. Death is peaceful.
It's the transition that's troublesome.

ISAAC ASIMOV

You don't get to choose how you're going to die.
Or when. You can only decide how
you're going to live.
Now.

JOAN BAEZ

THE BEST *Nonreligious* QUOTES EVER

Death does away with time.

SIMONE DE BEAUVOIR

Always go to other people's funerals, otherwise they won't come to yours.

YOGI BERRA

Death is nothing, but to live defeated and inglorious is to die daily.

NAPOLEON BONAPARTE

To live in the hearts we leave behind is not to die.

THOMAS CAMPBELL

Death is not the greatest loss in life. The greatest loss is what dies inside us while we live.

NORMAN COUSINS

Dream as if you'll live forever, live as if you'll die today.

JAMES DEAN

DEATH

That it will never come again
is what makes life so sweet.

EMILY DICKINSON

Our death is not an end if we can live on
in our children and the younger generation.
For they are us, our bodies are only wilted leaves
on the tree of life.

ALBERT EINSTEIN

Thus that which is the most awful of evils, death,
is nothing to us, since when we exist
there is no death,
and when there is death we do not exist.

EPICURUS

He who doesn't fear death dies only once.

GIOVANNI FALCONE

If I take death into my life, acknowledge it, and face
it squarely, I will free myself from the anxiety of
death and the pettiness of life — and only then
will I be free to become myself.

MARTIN HEIDEGGER

THE BEST *Nonreligious* QUOTES EVER

The world is a fine place and worth the fighting for
and I hate very much to leave it.

ERNEST HEMINGWAY

Many people die with their music still in them.
Why is this so? Too often it is because they are
always getting ready to live. Before they know it,
time runs out.

OLIVER WENDELL HOLMES

Do not take life too seriously.
You will never get out of it alive.

ELBERT HUBBARD

It is nothing to die; it is frightful not to live.

VICTOR HUGO

Death makes life meaningful.

NOELL HYMAN

DEATH

Remembering that you are going to die is the best way I know to avoid the trap of thinking you have something to lose. You are already naked. There is no reason not to follow your heart.

STEVE JOBS

There's something about death that is comforting. The thought that you could die tomorrow frees you to appreciate your life now.

ANGELINA JOLIE

You only live once — but if you work it right, once is enough.

JOE E. LEWIS

And in the end, it's not the years in your life that count. It's the life in your years.

ABRAHAM LINCOLN

I intend to live forever, or die trying.

GROUCHO MARX

THE BEST *Nonreligious* QUOTES EVER

There is nothing certain in a man's life
but that he must lose it.

OWEN MEREDITH

The idea is to die young as late as possible.

ASHLEY MONTAGU

People living deeply have no fear of death.

ANAIS NIN

Life is about not knowing, having to change,
taking the moment and making the best of it,
without knowing what's going to happen next.
Delicious Ambiguity.

GILDA RADNER

Once you have been confronted with a
life-and-death situation, trivia no longer matters.
Your perspective grows and
you live at a deeper level.
There's no time for pettiness.

MARGARETTA (HAPPY) ROCKEFELLER

DEATH

The fear of death follows from the fear of life.
A man who lives fully is prepared to die at any time.

MARK TWAIN

Let us so live that when we come to die
even the undertaker will be sorry.

MARK TWAIN

I didn't attend the funeral,
but I sent a nice letter saying I approved of it.

MARK TWAIN

Life is better than death, I believe,
if only because it is less boring,
and because it has fresh peaches in it.

ALICE WALKER

ENTHUSIASM

Do it no matter what. If you believe in it,
it is something very honorable. If somebody around
you or your family does not understand it, then
that's their problem. But if you do have a passion,
an honest passion, just do it.

MARIO ANDRETTI

It is not easy to find something that will intrigue
and bind your interest and enthusiasm.
This you must seek for yourself.

WALTER ANNENBERG

THE BEST *Nonreligious* QUOTES EVER

The condition of the most passionate enthusiast is to be preferred over the individual who, because of the fear of making a mistake, won't in the end affirm or deny anything.

THOMAS CARLYLE

Most great men and women are not perfectly rounded in their personalities, but are instead people whose one driving enthusiasm is so great it makes their faults seem insignificant.

CHARLES A. CERAMI

Enthusiasm is the greatest asset in the world. It beats money and power and influence.

HENRY CHESTER

Success consists of going from failure to failure without loss of enthusiasm.

WINSTON CHURCHILL

ENTHUSIASM

Nothing is so contagious as enthusiasm.

SAMUEL TAYLOR COLERIDGE

You will do foolish things,
but do them with enthusiasm.

COLETTE

My strength is my enthusiasm.

PLACIDO DOMINGO

Knowledge is power
and enthusiasm pulls the switch.

STEVE DROKE

I have not failed.
I've just found 10,000 ways
that won't work.

THOMAS EDISON

THE BEST *Nonreligious* QUOTES EVER

Nothing great was ever achieved
without enthusiasm.

RALPH WALDO EMERSON

I prefer the folly of enthusiasm
to the indifference of wisdom.

ANATOLE FRANCE

What I do best is share my enthusiasm.

BILL GATES

Carpe diem! Rejoice while you are alive;
enjoy the day; live life to the fullest;
make the most of what you have.
It is later than you think.

HORACE

The secret of genius is to carry the spirit of the child
into old age, which mean never losing
your enthusiasm.

ALDOUS HUXLEY

ENTHUSIASM

We act as though comfort and luxury
were the chief requirements of life,
when all that we need to make us happy is
something to be enthusiastic about.

CHARLES KINGLSEY

It is the greatest shot of adrenaline to be doing what
you've wanted to do so badly. You almost feel like
you could fly without the plane.

CHARLES LINDBERGH

If you aren't fired with enthusiasm,
you will be fired with enthusiasm.

VINCE LOMBARDI

Getting ahead in a difficult profession
requires avid faith in yourself. That is why
some people with mediocre talent,
but with great inner drive, go much further
than people with vastly superior talent.

SOPHIA LOREN

THE BEST *Nonreligious* QUOTES EVER

Years wrinkle the skin, but to give up enthusiasm wrinkles the soul.

GEN. DOUGLAS MACARTHUR

Earnestness is enthusiasm tempered by reason.

BLAISE PASCAL

Enthusiasm is everything.
It must be taut and vibrating like a guitar string.

PELE

A man can succeed at almost anything for which he has unlimited enthusiasm.

CHARLES M. SCHWAB

The measure of enthusiasm must be taken between interesting events. It is between bites that the lukewarm angler loses heart.

EDWIN WAY TEALE

ENTHUSIASM

None are so old as those
who have outlived enthusiasm.

HENRY DAVID THOREAU

As long as you're going to be thinking anyway,
think big.

DONALD TRUMP

Enthusiasm, like measles, mumps
and the common cold, is highly contagious.

EMORY WARD

If we're not enthusiastic, we can't get things done.
If we're over-enthusiastic, we run into the danger of
being fanatical.

WOODROW WYATT

A salesman minus enthusiasm is just a clerk.

AUTHOR UNKNOWN

FORGIVENESS

Our anger and annoyance are more detrimental
to us than the things themselves
which anger or annoy us.

MARCUS AURELIUS

It is easier to forgive an enemy than to
forgive a friend.

WILLIAM BLAKE

Nothing brings families together faster
than forgiveness.

DR. JOYCE BROTHERS

THE BEST *Nonreligious* QUOTES EVER

When we hate our enemies, we are giving them
power over us: power over our sleep, our appetites,
our blood pressure, our health and our happiness.
Our enemies would dance with joy if only they
knew how they were worrying us, lacerating us, and
getting even with us! Our hate is not hurting them
at all, but our hate is turning our days and nights
into a hellish turmoil.

DALE CARNEGIE

People can be more forgiving than you can imagine.
But you have to forgive yourself.
Let go of what's bitter and move on

BILL COSBY

Life is an adventure in forgiveness.

NORMAN COUSINS

For every minute you remain angry,
you give up sixty seconds of peace of mind.

RALPH WALDO EMERSON

FOREGIVENESS

Keeping score of old scores and scars, getting even
and one-upping, always makes you
less than you are.

MALCOLM FORBES

There's no point in burying the hatchet
if you're going to put up a marker on the site.

SYDNEY HARRIS

As long as you don't forgive, who and whatever it is
will occupy rent-free space in your mind.

ISABELLE HOLLAND

Forgive your enemies,
but never forget their names.

JOHN F. KENNEDY

Holding on to anger, resentment and hurt only
gives you tense muscles, a headache and a sore jaw
from clenching your teeth. Forgiveness gives you
back the laughter and the lightness in your life.

JOAN LUNDEN

THE BEST *Nonreligious* QUOTES EVER

Resentment is like taking poison and waiting for the other person to die.

MALACHY MCCOURT

When you forgive, you in no way change the past — but you sure do change the future.

BERNARD MELTZER

The more we know the better we forgive.
Whoever feels deeply, feels for all who live.

MADAME DE STAEL

The stupid neither forgive nor forget;
the naive forgive and forget; the wise forgive but do not forget.

THOMAS S. SZASZ

Forgiveness is the fragrance that the violet sheds on the heel that has crushed it.

MARK TWAIN

FOREGIVENESS

Love is an act of endless forgiveness,
a tender look which becomes a habit.

PETER USTINOV

To carry a grudge is like being stung to death
by one bee.

WILLIAM H. WALTON

Always forgive your enemies —
nothing annoys them so much.

OSCAR WILDE

It is better to ask forgiveness
than it is to ask permission.

AUTHOR UNKNOWN

FRIENDSHIP

Without friends no one would choose to live,
though he had all other goods.

ARISTOTLE

False friends are like our shadow, keeping close to
us while we walk in the sunshine, but leaving us
the instant we cross into the shade.

CHRISTIAN NEVELL BOVEE

If we would build on a sure foundation
in friendship, we must love friends
for their sake rather than for our own.

CHARLOTTE BRONTE

THE BEST *Nonreligious* QUOTES EVER

Remember that the most valuable antiques are dear old friends.

H. JACKSON BROWN, JR.

Friendship is like money, easier made than kept.

SAMUEL BUTLER

Don't walk in front of me, I may not follow.
Don't walk behind me, I may not lead.
Just walk beside me and be my friend.

ALBERT CAMUS

Treat your friends as you do your best pictures, and place them in their best light.

JENNIE JEROME CHURCHILL

What a delight it is to make friends with someone you have despised!

COLETTE

True friendship is like sound health; the value of it is seldom known until it be lost.

CHARLES CALEB COLTON

FRIENDSHIP

Friends are those rare people who ask how we are
and then wait to hear the answer.

ED CUNNINGHAM

It's the friends you can call up at 4:00 a.m.
that matter.

MARLENE DIETRICH

A friend may well be reckoned
the masterpiece of nature.

RALPH WALDO EMERSON

The only way to have a friend is to be one.

RALPH WALDO EMERSON

It is not so much our friends' help that helps us
as the confident knowledge that they will help us.

EPICURUS

Treasure each other in the recognition that
we do not know how long we shall have each other.

JOSHUA LOTH LIEBMAN

THE BEST *Nonreligious* QUOTES EVER

The best way to destroy an enemy is to
make him a friend.

ABRAHAM LINCOLN

Few delights can equal the mere presence of
someone we utterly trust.

GEORGE MACDONALD

A true friend is someone who thinks that you are a
good egg even though he knows that
you are slightly cracked.

BERNARD MELTZER

Hold a true friend with both hands.

NIGERIAN PROVERB

Each friend represents a world in us,
a world possibly not born until they arrive,
and it is only by this meeting that
a new world is born.

ANAIS NIN

FRIENDSHIP

We need old friends to help us grow old and new friends to help us stay young.

LETTIE COTTIN POGREBIN

Sometimes our light goes out but is blown into flame by another human being. Each of us owes deepest thanks to those who have rekindled this light.

ALBERT SCHWEITZER

Friendship doubles our joy and divides our grief.

SWEDISH PROVERB

No person is your friend
who demands your silence,
or denies your right to grow.

ALICE WALKER

Friendship is a plant of slow growth and must undergo and withstand the shocks of adversity before it is entitled to the appellation.

GEORGE WASHINGTON

THE BEST *Nonreligious* QUOTES EVER

I no doubt deserved my enemies,
but I don't believe I deserved my friends.

WALT WHITMAN

A real friend is one who walks in
when the rest of the world walks out.

WALTER WINCHELL

A friend hears the song in my heart
and sings it to me when my memory fails.

AUTHOR UNKNOWN

A real friend never gets in your way –
unless you happen to be on the way down.

AUTHOR UNKNOWN

True friendship comes when the silence
between two people is comfortable.

AUTHOR UNKNOWN

HAPPINESS

Now and then it's good to pause in our
pursuit of happiness and
just be happy.

GUILAUME APOLLINAIRE

It is only possible to live happily ever after
on a day to day basis.

MARGARET BONNANO

Happiness is having a large, loving,
caring, close-knit family
in another city.

GEORGE BURNS

THE BEST *Nonreligious* QUOTES EVER

That is happiness; to be dissolved into something completely great.

WILLA CATHER

The Grand essentials of happiness are: something to do, something to love, and something to hope for.

ALLAN CHALMERS

What a wonderful life I've had! I only wish I'd realized it sooner.

COLETTE

To find out what one is fitted to do, and to secure an opportunity to do it, is the key to happiness.

JOHN DEWEY

Happiness is like a butterfly which, when pursued, is always beyond our grasp, but, if you will sit down quietly, may alight upon you.

NATHANIEL HAWTHORNE

HAPPINESS

The supreme happiness of life is the conviction that
we are loved; loved for ourselves —
say rather, loved in spite of ourselves.

VICTOR HUGO

Happiness is not achieved by the conscious pursuit
of happiness; it is generally the by-product
of other activities.

ALDOUS HUXLEY

Even a happy life cannot be without a measure
of darkness, and the word 'happy' would lose its
meaning if it were not balanced by sadness.

CARL JUNG

When one door of happiness closes, another opens;
but often we look so long at the closed door that we
do not see the one which has been opened for us.

HELEN KELLER

Remember that as a teenager you are in the last
stage of your life when you will be happy to hear
the phone is for you.

FRAN LEIBOWITZ

THE BEST *Nonreligious* QUOTES EVER

Most folks are about as happy as they
make up their minds to be.

ABRAHAM LINCOLN

If you plan on being anything less than
you are capable of being, you will probably be
unhappy all the days of your life.

ABRAHAM MASLOW

I have learned to seek my happiness by limiting my
desires, rather than in attempting to satisfy them.

JOHN STUART MILL

The true secret of happiness lies in taking a genuine
interest in all the details of daily life.

WILLIAM MORRIS

Satisfaction of one's curiosity is one of the greatest
sources of happiness in life.

LINUS PAULING

HAPPINESS

The good life is a process, not a state of being.
It is a direction, not a destination.

CARL ROGERS

There is only one happiness in life,
to love and be loved.

GEORGE SAND

Happiness is nothing more than good health
and a bad memory.

ALBERT SCHWEITZER

Success is not the key to happiness. Happiness is
the key to success. If you love what you are doing,
you will be successful.

ALBERT SCHWEITZER

What can be added to the happiness of the man
who is in health, who is out of debt,
and has a clear conscience?

ADAM SMITH

THE BEST *Nonreligious* QUOTES EVER

There can be no happiness if the things we believe in are different from the things we do.

FREYA STARK

There is no duty we so underrate as the duty of being happy. By being happy we sow anonymous benefits upon the world.

ROBERT LOUIS STEVENSON

Life would be infinitely happier if we could only be born at the age of eighty and gradually approach eighteen.

MARK TWAIN

There is nothing which can better deserve our patronage than the promotion of science and literature. Knowledge is in every country the surest basis of public happiness.

GEORGE WASHINGTON

Some cause happiness wherever they go; others, whenever they go.

OSCAR WILDE

HAPPINESS

Success is getting what you want;
happiness is wanting what you get.

AUTHOR UNKNOWN

Enjoy the little things,
for one day you may look back
and realize they were the big things.

AUTHOR UNKNOWN

Dignity does not consist in possessing honors,
but in deserving them.

ARISTOTLE

Honor is like an island, rugged and without shores;
once we have left it, we can never return.

NICHOLAS BOILEAU

It takes 20 years to build a reputation
and five minutes to ruin it. If you think about that,
you'll do things differently.

WARREN BUFFETT

THE BEST *Nonreligious* QUOTES EVER

A hero is someone who has given his or her life to something bigger than oneself.

JOSEPH CAMPBELL

Show me the man you honor, and I will know what kind of man you are.

THOMAS CARLYLE

All honor's wounds are self-inflicted.

ANDREW CARNEGIE

Our own heart, and not other men's opinions, forms our true honor.

SAMUEL TAYLOR COLERIDGE

No person was ever honored for what he received. Honor has been the reward for what he gave.

CALVIN COOLIDGE

HONOR

Let no man turn aside, ever so slightly, from the broad path of honor, on the plausible pretence that he is justified by the goodness of his end. All good ends can be worked out by good means.

CHARLES DICKENS

The louder he talked of his honor, the faster we counted our spoons.

RALPH WALDO EMERSON

There are people who observe the rules of honor as we observe the stars: from a distance.

VICTOR HUGO

All tyranny needs to gain a foothold is for people of good conscience to remain silent.

THOMAS JEFFERSON

Justice of the right is always to take precedence over might.

BARBARA JORDAN

THE BEST *Nonreligious* QUOTES EVER

Those who give, hoping to be rewarded with honor, are not giving, they are bargaining.

PHILO JUDAEUS

A true man of honor feels humbled himself when he cannot help humbling others.

ROBERT E. LEE

A man has honor if he holds himself to an ideal of conduct though it is inconvenient, unprofitable, or dangerous to do so.

WALTER LIPPMANN

Always tell the truth — it's the easiest thing to remember.

DAVID MAMET

Those are my principles, and if you don't like them ... well, I have others.

GROUCHO MARX

Marriage: love, honor, and negotiate.

JOE MOORE

HONOR

Success without honor is an unseasoned dish;
it will satisfy your hunger, but it won't taste good.

JOE PATERNO

You can be deprived of your money, your job and
your home by someone else, but remember that
no one can ever take away your honor.

WILLIAM LYON PHELPS

Honor has not to be won; it must only not be lost.

ARTHUR SCHOPENHAUER

Mine honor is my life; both grow in one;
Take honor from me, and my life is done.

WILLIAM SHAKESPEARE

The most tragic thing in the world is
a man of genius who is not a man of honor.

GEORGE BERNARD SHAW

The greatest way to live with honor in this world is
to be what we pretend to be.

SOCRATES

THE BEST *Nonreligious* QUOTES EVER

Rather fail with honor than succeed by fraud.
SOPHOCLES

One of the common failings among honorable people is a failure to appreciate how thoroughly dishonorable some other people can be, and how dangerous it is to trust them.
THOMAS SOWELL

It is better to deserve honors and not have them than to have them and not deserve them.
MARK TWAIN

Character, not circumstances, makes the man.
BOOKER T. WASHINGTON

Real integrity is doing the right thing, knowing that nobody's going to know whether you did it or not.
OPRAH WINFREY

Three grand essentials to happiness in this life are something to do, something to love, and something to hope for.

JOSEPH ADDISON

So many tangles in life are ultimately hopeless that we have no appropriate sword other than laughter.

GORDON WILLIAM ALLPORT

No matter how happily a woman may be married, it always pleases her to discover that there is a really nice man who wishes she were not.

MARY CATHERINE BATESON

THE BEST *Nonreligious* QUOTES EVER

In the depths of winter, I finally learnt in me there was an invincible summer.

ALBERT CAMUS

While there's life, there's hope.

CICERO

The capacity for hope is the most significant fact of life. It provides human beings with a sense of destination and the energy to get started.

NORMAN COUSINS

Learn from yesterday, live for today, hope for tomorrow.

ALBERT EINSTEIN

I am not an optimist, because I am not sure that everything ends well. Nor am I a pessimist, because I am not sure that everything ends badly. I just carry hope in my heart.

VACLAV HAVEL

HOPE

It is the around-the-corner brand of hope that prompts people to action, while the distant hope acts as an opiate.

ERIC HOFFER

Beware how you take away hope from any human being.

OLIVER WENDELL HOLMES, JR.

Hope is the feeling that the feeling you have isn't permanent.

JEAN KERR

The very least you can do in your life is to figure out what you hope for. And the most you can do is live inside that hope.

BARBARA KINGSOLVER

Once you choose hope, anything's possible.

CHRISTOPHER REEVE

THE BEST *Nonreligious* QUOTES EVER

I have had dreams and I have had nightmares,
but I have conquered my nightmares
because of my dreams.

JONAS SALK

In the face of uncertainty, there is
nothing wrong with hope.

BERNIE S. SIEGEL

There is no hope unmingled with fear, and no fear
unmingled with hope.

BARUCH SPINOZA

The point of living and of being an optimist
is to be foolish enough to believe
the best is yet to come.

PETER USTINOV

Hope is like a road in the country:
there was never a road, but when many people walk
on it, the road comes into existence.

LIN YUTANG

HOPE

We are all in the gutter, but some of us are looking at the stars.

OSCAR WILDE

HUMOR

I love deadlines. I especially like the whooshing sound they make as they go flying by.

DOUGLAS ADAMS

We are here on earth to do good for others.
What the others are here for,
I don't know.

W.H. AUDEN

Imagination was given to man to compensate him for what he is not; a sense of humor to console him for what he is.

SIR FRANCIS BACON

THE BEST *Nonreligious* QUOTES EVER

Fishing is boring, unless you catch an actual fish, and then it is disgusting.

DAVE BARRY

Memory is the first casualty of middle age, if I remember correctly.

CANDICE BERGEN

If you come to a fork in the road, take it.

YOGI BERRA

It's like déjà vu all over again.

YOGI BERRA

You must never underestimate the power of the eyebrow.

JACK BLACK

When humor goes, there goes civilization.

ERMA BOMBECK

HUMOR

He is a self-made man and worships his creator.

JOHN BRIGHT

Too bad that all the people who really know how to run the country are busy driving taxi cabs and cutting hair.

GEORGE BURNS

Don't sweat the petty things and don't pet the sweaty things.

GEORGE CARLIN

There's so much comedy on television. Does that cause comedy in the streets?

DICK CAVETT

A fanatic is a person who can't change his mind and won't change the subject.

SIR WINSTON CHURCHILL

Love is a full-length mirror.

STEPHEN COLBERT

THE BEST *Nonreligious* QUOTES EVER

Imitation is the sincerest form of identity theft.

STEPHEN COLBERT

You can turn painful situations around
through laughter. If you can find humor
in anything, even poverty,
you can survive it.

BILL COSBY

I ask people why they have deer heads on their
walls. They always say because it's such a beautiful
animal. There you go. I think my mother is
attractive, but I have photographs of her.

ELLEN DEGENERES

My grandmother started walking five miles a day
when she was sixty. She's ninety-seven now,
and we don't know where the hell she is.

ELLEN DEGENERES

Personally, I have nothing against work, particularly
when performed, quietly and unobtrusively,
by someone else.

BARBARA EHRENREICH

HUMOR

Moderation in all things — including moderation.

BENJAMIN FRANKLIN

Where there's a will — there's a relative!

RICKY GERVAIS

I'd give my right arm to be ambidextrous.

GRAFFITI

Not only is life a bitch, it has puppies.

ADRIENNE GUSOFF

He had delusions of adequacy.

WALTER KERR

Christmas is a time when kids tell Santa what they want and adults pay for it. Deficits are when adults tell the government what they want and their kids pay for it.

RICHARD LAMM

THE BEST *Nonreligious* QUOTES EVER

USA Today has come out with a new survey:
Apparently three out of four people
make up 75 percent of the population.

DAVID LETTERMAN

Somewhere on this globe, every ten seconds,
there is a woman giving birth to a child.
She must be found and stopped.

SAM LEVENSON

A person reveals his character by nothing so clearly
as the joke he resents.

GEORG CHRISTOPHER LICHTENBERG

Curious people are interesting people;
I wonder why that is.

BILL MAHER

The secret of life is honesty and fair dealing.
If you can fake that, you've got it made.

GROUCHO MARX

HUMOR

The freedom of any society varies proportionately
with the volume of its laughter.

ZERO MOSTEL

You cannot hold back a good laugh
any more than you can the tide.
Both are forces of nature.

WILLIAM ROTSLER

Brevity is the soul of wit.

WILLIAM SHAKESPEARE

I often quote myself.
It adds spice to my conversation.

GEORGE BERNARD SHAW

When a thing is funny, search it carefully for
a hidden truth.

GEORGE BERNARD SHAW

THE BEST *Nonreligious* QUOTES EVER

Joy in one's heart and some laughter on one's lips
is a sign that the person down deep
has a pretty good grasp of life.

HUGH SIDEY

A bore is a man who, when you ask him how he is,
tells you.

BEERT LESTON TAYLOR

Humor is tragedy plus time.

MARK TWAIN

Humor is the great thing, the saving thing.
The minute it crops up, all our irritation and
resentments slip away, and a sunny
spirit takes their place.

MARK TWAIN

He has Van Gogh's ear for music.

BILLY WILDER

HUMOR

Everything in my life has been determined
by mistakes.

GENE WILDER

Ah, yes, divorce . . . from the Latin word meaning
to rip out a man's genitals through his wallet.

ROBIN WILLIAMS

Never trust a computer
you can't throw out a window.

STEVE WOZNIAK

When I get real bored, I like to drive downtown
and get a great parking spot, then sit in my car and
count how many people ask me if I'm leaving.

STEVEN WRIGHT

I was standing in the park wondering why frisbees
got bigger as they get closer.
Then it hit me.

AUTHOR UNKNOWN

KINDNESS

Life is short. Be swift to love!
Make haste to be kind!

HENRI F. AMIEL

From what we get, we can make a living;
what we give, however, makes a life.

ARTHUR ASHE

Always be a little kinder than necessary.

SIR JAMES M. BARRIE

THE BEST *Nonreligious* QUOTES EVER

A person who is nice to you, but rude to the waiter, is not a nice person.

DAVE BARRY

Real charity doesn't care if it's tax-deductible or not.

DAN BENNETT

Remember that everyone you meet is afraid of something, loves something and has lost something.

H. JACKSON BROWN, JR.

How far you go in life depends on your being tender with the young, compassionate with the aged, sympathetic with the striving and tolerant of the weak and strong. Because someday in your life you will have been all of these.

GEORGE WASHINGTON CARVER

A bit of fragrance always clings to the hand that gives roses.

CHINESE PROVERB

KINDNESS

The happiness of life is made up of minute fractions — the little, soon-forgotten charities of a kiss or smile, a kind look or heartfelt compliment.

SAMUEL TAYLOR COLERIDGE

The greatest good you can do for another
is not just to share your riches
but to reveal to him his own.

BENJAMIN DISRAELI

The greatest work that kindness does to others
is that it makes them kind themselves.

AMELIA EARHART

A fellow who does things that count,
doesn't usually stop to count them.

ALBERT EINSTEIN

You cannot do a kindness too soon,
for you never know how soon
it will be too late.

RALPH WALDO EMERSON

THE BEST *Nonreligious* QUOTES EVER

We have two ears and one mouth so that we can listen twice as much as we speak.

EPICTETUS

Something that has always puzzled me all my life is why, when I am in special need of help, the good deed is usually done by somebody on whom I have no claim.

WILLIAM FEATHER

The more sympathy you give, the less you need.

MALCOLM S. FORBES

Remember not only to say the right thing in the right place, but far more difficult still, to leave unsaid the wrong thing at the tempting moment.

BENJAMIN FRANKLIN

Be nice to nerds. Chances are you'll end up working for one.

BILL GATES

KINDNESS

Treat people as if they were what they ought to be,
and you help them to become
what they are capable of being.

GOETHE

Kindness can become its own motive.
We are made kind by being kind.

ERIC HOFFER

If you haven't any charity in your heart,
you have the worst kind of heart trouble.

BOB HOPE

Three things in human life are important:
The first is to be kind. The second is to be kind.
And the third is to be kind.

HENRY JAMES

Kindness is in our power,
even when fondness is not.

SAMUEL JOHNSON

THE BEST *Nonreligious* QUOTES EVER

There's no use doing a kindness
if you do it a day too late.

CHARLES KINGSLEY

I always prefer to believe the best of everybody,
it saves so much trouble.

RUDYARD KIPLING

The everyday kindness of the back roads more than
makes up for the acts of greed in the headlines.

CHARLES KURALT

If we could read the secret history of our enemies,
we should find in each man's life sorrow and
suffering enough to disarm all hostility.

HENRY WADSWORTH LONGFELLOW

Don't be yourself — be someone a little nicer.

MIGNON MCLAUGHLIN

If those who owe us nothing gave us nothing,
how poor we would be.

ANTONIO PORCHIA

KINDNESS

Be kind, for everyone you meet
is fighting a hard battle.

PLATO

Human kindness has never weakened the stamina
or softened the fiber of a free people.
A nation does not have to be cruel to be tough.

FRANKLIN D. ROOSEVELT

Compassion is the basis of all morality.

ARTHUR SCHOPENHAUER

Constant kindness can accomplish much.
As the sun makes ice melt, kindness causes
misunderstanding, mistrust, and hostility
to evaporate.

ALBERT SCHWEITZER

Wherever there is a human being,
there is an opportunity for kindness.

SENECA

THE BEST *Nonreligious* QUOTES EVER

Love all. Trust a few. Do wrong to none.
WILLIAM SHAKESPEARE

Kindness, I've discovered, is everything in life.
ISAAC BASHEVIS SINGER

Kindness is the language which the deaf can hear
and the blind can see.
MARK TWAIN

If you stop to be kind,
you must swerve often from your path.
MARY WEBB

You can't live a perfect day without doing
something for someone who will
never be able to repay you.
JOHN WOODEN

What the world really needs is more love
and less paperwork.

PEARL BAILEY

Whoever said love is blind is dead wrong. Love is
the only thing that lets us see each other
with the remotest accuracy.

MARTHA BECK

Take away love and our earth is a tomb.

ROBERT BROWNING

THE BEST *Nonreligious* QUOTES EVER

You have to walk carefully in the beginning of love;
the running across fields into your lover's arms
can only come later when you're sure
they won't laugh if you trip.

JONATHAN CARROLL

It is a curious thought, but it is only when you see
people looking ridiculous that you realize
just how much you love them.

AGATHA CHRISTIE

There's only two things that money can't buy, and
that's true love and homegrown tomatoes.

GUY CLARK

Nobody has ever measured, not even poets, how
much the human heart can hold.

ZELDA FITZGERALD

One is very crazy when in love.

SIGMUND FREUD

LOVE

Love is an irresistible desire to be irresistibly desired.

ROBERT FROST

Love is a condition in which the happiness of another person is essential to your own.

ROBERT HEINLEIN

Love has nothing to do with what you are expecting to get — only with what you are expecting to give — which is everything.

KATHARINE HEPBURN

Love doesn't just sit there like a stone, it has to be made, like brick; re-made all the time, made new.

URSALA K. LE GUIN

The great tragedy of life is not that men perish, but that they cease to love.

SOMERSET MAUGHAM

THE BEST *Nonreligious* QUOTES EVER

Love is like war: easy to begin but very hard to stop.

H. L. MENCKEN

The one thing we can never get enough of is love.
And the one thing we never give enough of is love.

HENRY MILLER

If you live to be a hundred,
I want to live to be a hundred minus one day
so I never have to live without you.

A. A. MILNE

Love that stammers, that stutters,
is apt to be the love that loves best.

GABRIELA MISTRAL

Those who love deeply never grow old;
they may die of old age, but they die young.

SIR ARTHUR WING PINERO

Falling in love and having a relationship
are two different things.

KEANU REEVES

LOVE

To fear love is to fear life, and those who fear life are already three parts dead.

BERTRAND RUSSELL

For small creatures such as we the vastness is bearable only through love.

CARL SAGAN

Love does not consist of gazing at one another, but in looking outward in the same direction.

ANTOINE DE SAINT-EXUPERY

Love conquers all.

VIRGIL

Love is a canvas furnished by nature and embroidered by imagination.

VOLTAIRE

Who, being loved, is poor?

OSCAR WILDE

MEANING AND PURPOSE

We must put people at the center
of everything we do. No calling is more noble,
and no responsibility greater, than that
of enabling men, women and children,
in cities and in villages around the world,
to make their lives better.

KOFI ANNAN

If you don't know where you are going,
you might wind up someplace else.

YOGI BERRA

Follow your bliss and doors will open
where there were no doors before.

JOSEPH CAMPBELL

THE BEST *Nonreligious* QUOTES EVER

We make a living by what we get,
but we make a life by what we give.

WINSTON CHURCHILL

No one can give you better advice than yourself.

CICERO

Nothing in life is to be feared.
It is only to be understood.

MARIE CURIE

Life itself is just a thin coat of paint on the planet,
and we hold the paintbrush.

DANIEL DENNETT

What do we live for, if it is not to make life
less difficult for each other?

GEORGE ELIOT

MEANING AND PURPOSE

To laugh often and much; to win the respect of
intelligent people and the affection of children . . .
to leave the world a better place . . . to know even
one life has breathed easier because you have lived.
This is to have succeeded.

RALPH WALDO EMERSON

What is the end of human life? It is not, believe me,
the chief end of man that he should make a fortune
and beget children whose end is likewise to make a
fortune, but it is, in few words, that
he should explore himself.

RALPH WALDO EMERSON

Millions long for immortality who do not know
what to do with themselves
on a rainy Sunday afternoon.

SUSAN ERTZ

Everything can be taken from a man but . . . the last
of the human freedoms — to choose one's attitude
in any given set of circumstances,
to choose one's own way.

VIKTOR FRANKL

THE BEST *Nonreligious* QUOTES EVER

Hide not your talents. They for use were made.
What's a sundial in the shade?

BENJAMIN FRANKLIN

As soon as you trust yourself,
you will know how to live.

GOETHE

Work for something because it is good,
not just because it stands a chance to succeed.

VACLAV HAVEL

The best thing to hold onto in life is each other.

AUDREY HEPBURN

Great minds have purposes, others have wishes.

WASHINGTON IRVING

Actually, this seems to be the basic need of the
human heart in nearly every great crisis
— a good hot cup of coffee.

ALEXANDER KING

MEANING AND PURPOSE

Time you enjoy wasting, was not wasted.

JOHN LENNON

Life is a whim of several billion cells
to be you for a while.

GROUCHO MARX

Never doubt that a small group of thoughtful,
committed citizens can change the world; indeed,
it's the only thing that ever has.

MARGARET MEAD

Some people walk in the rain, others just get wet.

ROGER MILLER

Tell me, what is it you plan to do with your one
wild and precious life?

MARY OLIVER

Man, a being in search of meaning.

PLATO

THE BEST *Nonreligious* QUOTES EVER

Half our life is spent trying to find something to do with the time we have rushed through life trying to save.

WILL ROGERS

Our lives teach us who we are.

SALMAN RUSHDIE

Time is the coin of your life. It is the only coin you have, and only you can determine how it will be spent. Be careful lest you let other people spend it for you.

CARL SANDBURG

It is only with the heart that one can see rightly; what is essential is invisible to the eye.

ANTOINE DE SAINT-EXUPERY

Some men see things as they are and say, "Why?" I dream of things that never were and say, "Why not?"

GEORGE BERNARD SHAW

MEANING AND PURPOSE

The unexamined life is not worth living.

SOCRATES

We can tell our values by looking
at our checkbook stubs.

GLORIA STEINEM

If a man does not keep pace with his companions, perhaps it is because he hears a different drummer. Let him step to the music which he hears, however measured or far away.

HENRY DAVID THOREAU

Many men go fishing all of their lives without knowing it is not fish they are after.

HENRY DAVID THOREAU

Twenty years from now you will be more disappointed by the things you didn't do than by the ones you did do. So throw off the bowlines. Sail away from the safe harbor. Catch the trade winds in your sails. Explore. Dream. Discover.

MARK TWAIN

THE BEST *Nonreligious* QUOTES EVER

The key to wisdom is not how much you know, but how well you understand how little you know.

MARK VERNON

The man of character, sensitive to the meaning of what he is doing, will know how to discover the ethical paths in the maze of possible behavior.

EARL WARREN

If I asked for a cup of coffee, someone would search for the double meaning.

MAE WEST

To live is the rarest thing in the world. Most people exist, that is all.

OSCAR WILDE

Nature is our chapel.

BJORK

Man masters nature not by force
but by understanding.

JACOB BROWNOWSKI

It is good to know our universe.
What is new is only new to us.

PEARL S. BUCK

THE BEST *Nonreligious* QUOTES EVER

A flower is an educated weed.

LUTHER BURBANK

I go to nature to be soothed and healed, and to have my senses put in order.

JOHN BURROUGHS

Those who dwell among the beauties and mysteries of the earth are never alone or weary of life.

RACHEL CARSON

Let us learn to appreciate there will be times when the trees will be bare, and look forward to the time when we may pick the fruit.

ANTON CHEKHOV

Whoever loves and understands a garden will find contentment within.

CHINESE PROVERB

NATURE

Look deep into nature, and then
you will understand everything better.

ALBERT EINSTEIN

The earth laughs in flowers.

RALPH WALDO EMERSON

Adopt the pace of nature: her secret is patience.

RALPH WALDO EMERSON

Now there is one outstandingly important fact
regarding Spaceship Earth, and that is that
no instruction book came with it.

BUCKMINSTER FULLER

The sun, with all those planets revolving around it
and dependent upon it, can still ripen a bunch of
grapes as if it had nothing else in the universe to do.

GALILEO

THE BEST *Nonreligious* QUOTES EVER

The natural world is dynamic. From the expanding universe to the hair on a baby's head, nothing is the same from now to the next moment.

HELEN HOOVER

There are in nature
neither rewards nor punishments —
there are only consequences.

ROBERT G. INGERSOLL

Fall is my favorite season in Los Angeles, watching the birds change color and fall from the trees.

DAVID LETTERMAN

There are always flowers for those
who want to see them.

HENRI MATISSE

Nature always takes her time. Great oaks don't become great overnight. They also lose a lot of leaves, branches and bark in the process of becoming great.

ANDREW MATTHEWS

NATURE

There are no passengers on spaceship earth.
We are all crew.

MARSHALL MCLUHAN

I perhaps owe having become a painter to flowers.

CLAUDE MONET

In every walk with nature one receives far more
than he seeks.

JOHN MUIR

People from a planet without flowers would think
we must be mad with joy the whole time
to have such things about us.

IRIS MURDOCH

And the day came when the risk to remain tight in
a bud was more painful than the risk
it took to blossom.

ANAIS NIN

THE BEST *Nonreligious* QUOTES EVER

Nature is an infinite sphere of which the center is everywhere and the circumference nowhere.

BLAISE PASCAL

Climb up on some hill at sunrise. Everybody needs perspective once in a while, and you'll find it there.

ROBB SAGENDORPH

If thou live according to nature, thou wilt never be poor; if according to the opinions of the world, thou wilt never be rich.

SENECA

It is not so much for its beauty that the forest makes a claim upon men's hearts, as for that subtle something, that quality of air that emanation from old trees, that so wonderfully changes and renews a weary spirit.

ROBERT LOUIS STEVENSON

Nature's music is never over; her silences are pauses, not conclusions.

MARY WEBB

NATURE

Come forth into the light of things,
let nature be your teacher.

WILLIAM WORDSWORTH

Study nature, love nature, stay close to nature.
It will never fail you.

FRANK LLOYD WRIGHT

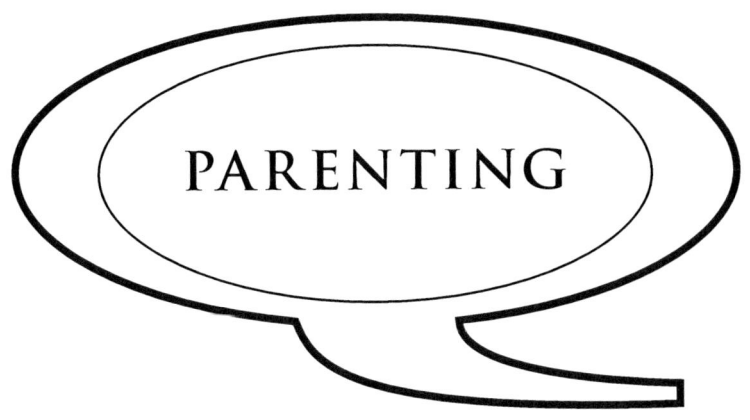

PARENTING

Raising kids is part joy and part guerilla warfare.

ED ASNER

When my kids become wild and unruly,
I use a nice, safe playpen. When they're finished,
I climb out.

ERMA BOMBECK

If a child is to keep alive his inborn sense of wonder, he needs the companionship of at least one adult who can share it, rediscovering with him the joy, excitement and mystery of the world we live in.

RACHEL CARSON

THE BEST *Nonreligious* QUOTES EVER

Human beings are the only creatures on earth that allow their children to come back home.

BILL COSBY

Kids spell love T-I-M-E.

JOHN CRUDELE

When I was a kid my parents moved a lot, but I always found them.

RODNEY DANGERFIELD

Being considerate of others will take your children further in life than any college degree.

MARIAN WRIGHT EDELMAN

Love and respect are the most important aspects of parenting, and of all relationships.

JODIE FOSTER

PARENTING

If you want your children to improve, let them
overhear the nice things you say about them
to others.

HAIM GINOTT

There is always one moment in childhood when
the door opens and lets the future in.

GRAHAM GREENE

It behooves a father to be blameless
if he expects his child to be.

HOMER

I believe we should encourage children to sing and
play instruments from an early age.

MICK JAGGER

Tell your kids the truth as you see it and let the
marketplace of ideas work
as they grow up.

PENN JILLETTE

THE BEST *Nonreligious* QUOTES EVER

If there is anything that we wish to change in the child, we should first examine it and see whether it is not something that could better be changed in ourselves.

CARL JUNG

The answer 'I don't know' is one of the greatest gifts a parent can give to a child's intellectual development. It is an answer both honest and too seldom heard.

ROBERT E. KAY

If you bungle raising your children, I don't think whatever else you do matters very much.

JACQUELINE KENNEDY ONASSIS

You have a lifetime to work, but children are only young once.

POLISH PROVERB

Children reinvent your world for you.

SUSAN SARANDON

PARENTING

If your kids are giving you a headache,
follow the directions on the aspirin bottle,
especially the part that says
"keep away from children."

SUSAN SAVANNAH

The child supplies the power
but the parents have to do the steering.

BENJAMIN SPOCK

Childbirth is more admirable than conquest,
more amazing than self-defense, and
as courageous as either one.

GLORIA STEINEM

I have found the best way to give advice to your
children is to find out what they want and then
advise them to do it.

HARRY S TRUMAN

If you want children to keep their feet on the
ground, put some responsibility on their shoulders.

ABIGAIL VAN BUREN

THE BEST *Nonreligious* QUOTES EVER

Any child can tell you that the sole purpose of a middle name is so he can tell when he's really in trouble.

AUTHOR UNKNOWN

A child enters your home and for the next twenty years makes so much noise you can hardly stand it. The child departs, leaving the house so silent you think you are going mad.

AUTHOR UNKNOWN

He who lives in harmony with himself
lives in harmony with the universe.

MARCUS AURELIUS

My therapist told me the way to achieve true inner
peace is to finish what I start. So far today, I have
finished 2 bags of M&M's and a chocolate cake.
I feel better already.

DAVE BARRY

A large part of the problem in the world today is
that the people who start wars do not fight in them.
If they did, we would have fewer wars.

DAVID CHRISTIE

THE BEST *Nonreligious* QUOTES EVER

For peace of mind, we need to resign as general manager of the universe.

LARRY EISENBERG

Peace and justice are two sides of the same coin.

DWIGHT D. EISENHOWER

Nothing can bring you peace but yourself.

RALPH WALDO EMERSON

Peace is not the product of a victory or a command. It has no finishing line, no final deadline, no fixed definition of achievement. Peace is a never-ending process, the work of many decisions.

OSCAR HAMMERSTEIN

All we are saying is give peace a chance.

JOHN LENNON

PEACE

Only in quiet waters do things mirror themselves undistorted. Only in a quiet mind is adequate perception of the world.

HANS MARGOLIUS

Until you make peace with who you are, you'll never be content with what you have.

DORIS MORTMAN

For it isn't enough to talk about peace. One must believe it. And it isn't enough to believe in it. One must work at it.

ELEANOR ROOSEVELT

Until he extends his circle of compassion to include all living things, man will not himself find peace.

ALBERT SCHWEITZER

PERSEVERANCE

Perseverance is failing 19 times
and succeeding the 20th.

JULIE ANDREWS

Pain is temporary. Quitting lasts forever.

LANCE ARMSTRONG

Look at life through the windshield,
not the rear-view mirror.

BYRD BAGGETT

THE BEST *Nonreligious* QUOTES EVER

It ain't over till it's over.

YOGI BERRA

My heroes are the ones who survived
doing it wrong, who made mistakes,
but recovered from them.

BONO

Victory belongs to the most persevering.

NAPOLEON BONAPARTE

If you wait to do everything
until you're sure it's right,
you'll probably never
do much of anything.

WIN BORDEN

Most of the important things in the world have
been accomplished by people who kept on trying
where there seemed to be no hope at all.

DALE CARNEGIE

PERSEVERANCE

Never give in! Never give in! Never, never, never, never — in nothing great or small, large or petty. Never give in except to convictions of honor and good sense.

WINSTON CHURCHILL

It does not matter how slowly you go so long as you do not stop.

CONFUCIUS

A champion is someone who gets up, even when he can't.

JACK DEMPSEY

Nearly every man who develops an idea works at it up to the point where it looks impossible, and then gets discouraged. That's not the place to become discouraged.

THOMAS EDISON

THE BEST *Nonreligious* QUOTES EVER

It's not that I'm so smart, it's just that
I stay with problems longer.

ALBERT EINSTEIN

The great majority of men are
bundles of beginnings.

RALPH WALDO EMERSON

Vitality shows in not only the ability to persist but
the ability to start over.

F. SCOTT FITZGERALD

One may go a long way after one is tired.

FRENCH PROVERB

In three words I can sum up everything
I've learned about life: it goes on.

ROBERT FROST

It's fine to celebrate success but it is more important
to heed the lessons of failure.

BILL GATES

PERSEVERANCE

In the realm of ideas everything depends on enthusiasm . . . in the real world all rests on perseverance.

GOETHE

Never measure the height of a mountain until you have reached the top. Then you will see how low it was.

DAG HAMMARSKJOLD

When I hear somebody sigh that "Life is hard," I am always tempted to ask, "Compared to what?"

SIDNEY J. HARRIS

As a man believes, so he will act.

SAM HARRIS

Intelligence is the ability to adapt to change.

STEVEN HAWKING

THE BEST *Nonreligious* QUOTES EVER

Most people never run far enough on their first wind to find out they've got a second.

WILLIAM JAMES

Expect trouble as an inevitable part of life and repeat to yourself, the most comforting words of all; this, too, shall pass.

ANN LANDERS

It's not whether you get knocked down; it's whether you get up.

VINCE LOMBARDI

We are not retreating — we are advancing in another direction.

DOUGLAS MACARTHUR

It always seems impossible until it's done.

NELSON MANDELA

Big shots are only little shots who keep shooting.

CHRISTOPHER MORLEY

PERSEVERANCE

You need to overcome the tug of people against you
as you reach for high goals.

GEORGE S. PATTON

He conquers who endures.

PERSIUS

The question isn't who is going to let me;
it's who is going to stop me.

AYN RAND

I do not think there is any other quality
so essential to success of any kind
as the quality of perseverance.
It overcomes almost everything,
even nature.

JOHN D. ROCKEFELLER

A man either lives life as it happens to him,
meets it head-on and licks it, or
he turns his back on it and
starts to wither away.

GENE RODDENBERRY

THE BEST *Nonreligious* QUOTES EVER

Scar tissue is stronger than regular tissue.
Realize the strength, move on.

HENRY ROLLINS

When you come to the end of your rope,
tie a knot and hang on.

FRANKLIN D. ROOSEVELT

It's hard to beat a person who never gives up.

BABE RUTH

Both now and for always, I intend to hold fast
to my belief in the hidden strength
of the human spirit.

ANDREI SAKHAROV

A lost battle is a battle one thinks one has lost.

JEAN-PAUL SARTRE

Only the guy who isn't rowing
has time to rock the boat.

JEAN-PAUL SARTRE

PERSEVERANCE

Don't give up. Don't ever give up.

JIM VALVANO

The violets in the mountains have broken the rocks.

TENNESSEE WILLIAMS

Don't be discouraged.
It's often the last key in the bunch that
opens the lock.

AUTHOR UNKNOWN

The darkest hour is just before the dawn.

AUTHOR UNKNOWN

The greatest oak was once a little nut
who held its ground.

AUTHOR UNKNOWN

When your dreams turn to dust, vacuum.

AUTHOR UNKNOWN

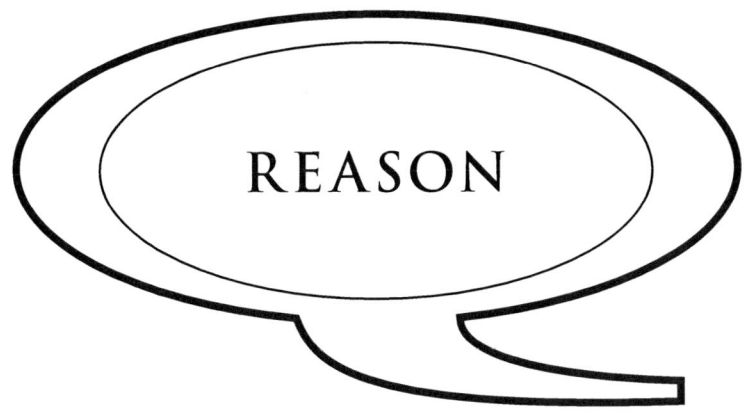

REASON

The freethinking of one age is the common sense of the next.

MATTHEW ARNOLD

Where so many hours have been spent in convincing myself that I am right, is there not some reason to fear I may be wrong?

JANE AUSTEN

Losing an illusion makes you wiser than finding a truth.

LUDWIG BORNE

THE BEST *Nonreligious* QUOTES EVER

I mean, in the most literal sense of the words, of course everything happens for a reason — if by "for a reason" you mean "as a result of cause and effect."

GRETA CHRISTINA

Faith is belief in spite of, even perhaps because of, the lack of evidence.

RICHARD DAWKINS

People believe things simply because people have believed the same things over the centuries.

RICHARD DAWKINS

If you would be a real seeker after truth, it is necessary that at least once in your life you doubt, as far as possible, all things.

RENE DESCARTES

Skepticism: the mark and even the pose of the educated mind.

JOHN DEWEY

REASON

He who will not reason is a bigot;
he who cannot is a fool; and
he who dares not is a slave.

WILLIAM DRUMMOND

The trouble with most people is that they think
with their hopes or fears or wishes
rather than with their minds.

WILL DURANT

Increasingly constructive doubt
is the sign of advancing civilization.

JEROME D. FRANK

If you will not hear Reason, she will surely
rap your knuckles.

BENJAMIN FRANKLIN

The most erroneous stories are those
we think we know best — and therefore
never scrutinize or question.

STEPHEN JAY GOULD

THE BEST *Nonreligious* QUOTES EVER

Heresy is only another word for freedom of thought.

GRAHAM GREENE

It is a thousand times better to have common sense without education than to have education without common sense.

ROBERT G. INGERSOLL

How many legs does a dog have if you call the tail a leg? Four. Calling a tail a leg doesn't make it a leg.

ABRAHAM LINCOLN

You can fool some of the people all of the time, and all of the people some of the time, but you cannot fool all of the people all of the time.

ABRAHAM LINCOLN

Men are never so likely to settle a question rightly as when they discuss it freely.

THOMAS BABINGTON MACAULAY

REASON

A good head and a good heart are always
a formidable combination.

NELSON MANDELA

He who establishes his argument by noise and
command shows that his reason is weak.

MICHEL EYQUEM DE MONTAIGNE

We must not confuse dissent with disloyalty.

EDWARD R. MURROW

If everyone is thinking alike,
then somebody isn't thinking.

GEORGE S. PATTON

The most formidable weapon against errors of
every kind is reason. I have never used any other,
and I trust I never shall.

THOMAS PAINE

THE BEST *Nonreligious* QUOTES EVER

No rational argument will have a rational effect on
a man who does not want to adopt
a rational attitude.

KARL POPPER

Reason is not automatic. Those who deny it cannot
be conquered by it. Do not count on them.
Leave them alone.

AYN RAND

Most of our so-called reasoning consists in finding
arguments for going on believing as we already do.

JAMES HARVEY ROBINSON

Not to be absolutely certain is, I think,
one of the essential things in rationality.

BERTRAND RUSSELL

It is far better to grasp the universe as it really is
than to persist in delusion,
however satisfying and reassuring.

CARL SAGAN

REASON

The truth is often a mixed message.

DAN SAVAGE

All truth passes through three stages. First, it is ridiculed. Second, it is violently opposed. Third, it is accepted as being self-evident.

ARTHUR SCHOPENHAUER

The fact that a believer is happier than a skeptic is no more to the point than the fact that a drunken man is happier than a sober one.

GEORGE BERNARD SHAW

The reasonable man adapts himself to the world; the unreasonable one persists in trying to adapt the world to himself. Therefore, all progress depends on the unreasonable man.

GEORGE BERNARD SHAW

Myths are stories that express meaning, morality or motivation. Whether they are true or not is irrelevant.

MICHAEL SHERMER

THE BEST *Nonreligious* QUOTES EVER

If I look over my life, every single step of maturing
for me, every single one, has had the
exact same common denominator,
and that was accepting what was true
over what I wished were true.

JULIA SWEENEY

Reason consists in constantly perceiving things
as they really are.

VOLTAIRE

Most of us can read the writing on the wall;
we just assume it's addressed to someone else.

IVERN BALL

I resolved to stop accumulating and begin the
infinitely more serious and difficult task
of wise distribution.

ANDREW CARNEGIE

The price of greatness is responsibility.

WINSTON CHURCHILL

THE BEST *Nonreligious* QUOTES EVER

I don't see the point of being a human being if you're not going to be responsible to your fellow human beings. Selfishness thefts away the human and reduces you to just a being.

CANDEA CORE-STARKE

Only do what your heart tells you.

PRINCESS DIANA

The willingness to accept responsibility for one's own life is the source from which self-respect springs.

JOAN DIDION

Don't waste life in doubts and fears; spend yourself on the work before you, well assured that the right performance of this hour's duties will be the best preparation for the hours and ages that will follow it.

RALPH WALDO EMERSON

RESPONSIBILITY

Well done is better than well said.
BENJAMIN FRANKLIN

Blaming mother is just a negative way
of clinging to her still.
NANCY FRIDAY

Until we're educating every kid in a fantastic way,
until every inner city is cleaned up,
there is no shortage of things to do.
BILL GATES

With every civil right there has to be
a corresponding civil obligation.
EDISON HAINES

Facts do not cease to exist because they are ignored.
ALDOUS HUXLEY

THE BEST *Nonreligious* QUOTES EVER

A new position of responsibility will usually show a
man to be a far stronger creature
than was supposed.

WILLIAM JAMES

Take your life in your own hands, and what
happens? A terrible thing: no one to blame.

ERICA JONG

If the society today allows wrongs to go
unchallenged, the impression is created that those
wrongs have the approval of the majority.

BARBARA JORDAN

I am only one; but still I am one.
I cannot do everything,
but still I can do something;
I will not refuse to do something I can do.

HELEN KELLER

RESPONSIBILITY

When we truly care for ourselves,
it becomes possible to care
far more profoundly about other people.

EDA LESHAN

You cannot escape the responsibility of tomorrow
by evading it today.

ABRAHAM LINCOLN

We have the Bill of Rights. What we need is a
Bill of Responsibilities.

BILL MAHER

Think of giving not as a duty but as a privilege.

JOHN D. ROCKEFELLER JR.

When will our consciences grow so tender that we
will act to prevent human misery
rather than avenge it?

ELEANOR ROOSEVELT

THE BEST *Nonreligious* QUOTES EVER

A sense of duty is useful in work, but offensive in
personal relations. People wish to be liked,
not be endured with patient resignation.

BERTRAND RUSSELL

We are made wise not by the recollection of our
past, but by the responsibility for our future.

GEORGE BERNARD SHAW

It is more rewarding to watch money change the
world than watch it accumulate.

GLORIA STEINEM

It is our responsibilities, not ourselves,
that we should take seriously.

PETER USTINOV

No snowflake in an avalanche ever feels responsible.

VOLTAIRE

RESPONSIBILITY

Few things help an individual more
than to place responsibility upon him,
and to let him know that you trust him.

BOOKER T. WASHINGTON

We all participate in weaving the social fabric;
we should therefore all participate in
patching the fabric when it develops holes.

ANNE C. WEISBERG

I don't think of myself as a poor deprived ghetto
girl who made good. I think of myself as
somebody who from an early age knew
I was responsible for myself, and
I had to make good.

OPRAH WINFREY

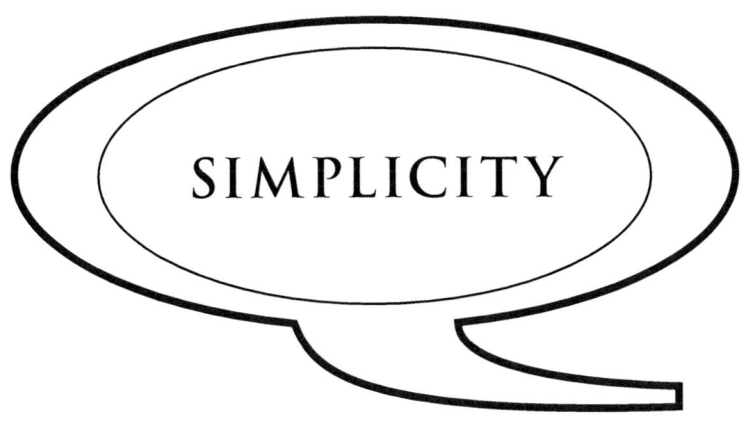

SIMPLICITY

Remember, you're the one who creates speed,
because you're the one who allows
stuff to enter your life.

DAVID ALLEN

The great artist and thinker are the simplifiers.

HENRI FREDERIC AMIEL

Nothing matters very much and
few things matter at all.

ARTHUR BALFOUR

THE BEST *Nonreligious* QUOTES EVER

During the great storms of our lives we imitate
those captains who jettison their weightiest cargo.

HONORE DE BALZAC

If you can't write your idea on the back of my
calling card, you don't have a clear idea.

DAVID BELASCO

Life is really simple,
but we insist on making it complicated.

CONFUCIUS

Simplicity is the ultimate sophistication.

LEONARDO DA VINCI

Everything should be made as simple as possible,
but not simpler.

ALBERT EINSTEIN

SIMPLICITY

The essence of philosophy is that a man should so
live that his happiness shall depend
as little as possible on external things.

EPICTETUS

Simplicity, carried to an extreme, becomes elegance.

JON FRANKLIN

Simplicity of character is the natural result
of profound thought.

WILLIAM HAZLITT

The ability to simplify means to
eliminate the unnecessary so that
the necessary may speak.

HANS HOFMANN

You have succeeded in life when all you really want
is only what you really need.

VERNON HOWARD

THE BEST *Nonreligious* QUOTES EVER

Making the simple complicated is commonplace; making the complicated simple, awesomely simple, that's creativity.

CHARLES MINGUS

The simplest things give me ideas.

JOAN MIRO

The simple act of paying attention can take you a long way.

KEANU REEVES

Too many people spend money they haven't earned, to buy things they don't want, to impress people they don't like.

WILL ROGERS

Any intelligent fool can make things bigger, more complex, and more violent. It takes a touch of genius — and a lot of courage — to move in the opposite direction.

E.F. SCHUMACKER

SIMPLICITY

In the hope of reaching the moon men fail to see
the flowers that blossom at their feet.

ALBERT SCHWEITZER

Simplicity, simplicity, simplicity!
I say, let your affairs be as two or three, and
not a hundred or a thousand.... Simplify, simplify.

HENRY DAVID THOREAU

When an idea is too weak to support a simple
statement, it is a sign that it should be rejected.

MARQUIS DE VAUVENARGUES

The wisdom of life consists in the
elimination of non-essentials.

LIN YUTANG

TOLERANCE

To be one, to be united is a great thing.
But to respect the right to be different
is maybe even greater.

BONO

I have seen great intolerance shown
in support of tolerance.

SAMUEL TAYLOR COLERIDGE

Human diversity makes tolerance more than a
virtue; it makes it a requirement for survival.

RENE DUBOS

THE BEST *Nonreligious* QUOTES EVER

The responsibility of tolerance lies with those
who have the wider vision.

GEORGE ELIOT

Being tolerant does not mean that I share another
one's belief. But it does mean that I acknowledge
another one's right to believe, and obey,
his own conscience.

VIKTOR FRANKL

Before you criticize someone, you should walk a
mile in their shoes. That way when
you criticize them, you are a mile away from them
and you have their shoes.

JACK HANDEY

Intolerance is the most socially acceptable form
of egotism, for it permits us to assume superiority
without personal boasting.

SIDNEY J. HARRIS

TOLERANCE

The self-respecting individual will try to be as
tolerant of his neighbor's shortcomings
as he is of his own.

ERIC HOFFER

Tolerance is giving to every other human being
every right that you claim for yourself.

ROBERT G. INGERSOLL

Tolerance implies no lack of commitment to one's
own beliefs. Rather it condemns the
oppression or persecution of others.

JOHN F. KENNEDY

I believe with all my heart that civilization has
produced nothing finer than a man or woman who
thinks and practices true tolerance.

FRANK KNOX

We must give ourselves a good hard mental swat
every time we feel inclined to mock, sneer, or roll
our eyes at those whose beliefs differ from our own.

DALE MCGOWAN

THE BEST *Nonreligious* QUOTES EVER

The price of the democratic way of life is a growing appreciation of people's differences, not merely as tolerable, but as the essence of a rich and rewarding human experience.

JEROME NATHANSON

You have your way. I have my way. As for the right way, the correct way, and the only way, it does not exist.

FRIEDRICH NIETZSCHE

I used to think anyone doing anything weird was weird. Now I know that it is the people that call others weird that are weird.

PAUL MCCARTNEY

Collective fear stimulates herd instinct, and tends to produce ferocity toward those who are not regarded as members of the herd.

BERTRAND RUSSELL

TOLERANCE

There are weapons that are simply thoughts.
For the record, prejudices can kill
and suspicion can destroy.

ROD SERLING

Think for yourselves and let others enjoy
the privilege to do so, too.

VOLTAIRE

Printed in the United States
119951LV00001B/1-162/P